Mexican Girls

Hot Sexy Mexican Lingerie Girls Models Pictures

By **PHOTO ART LOVER**

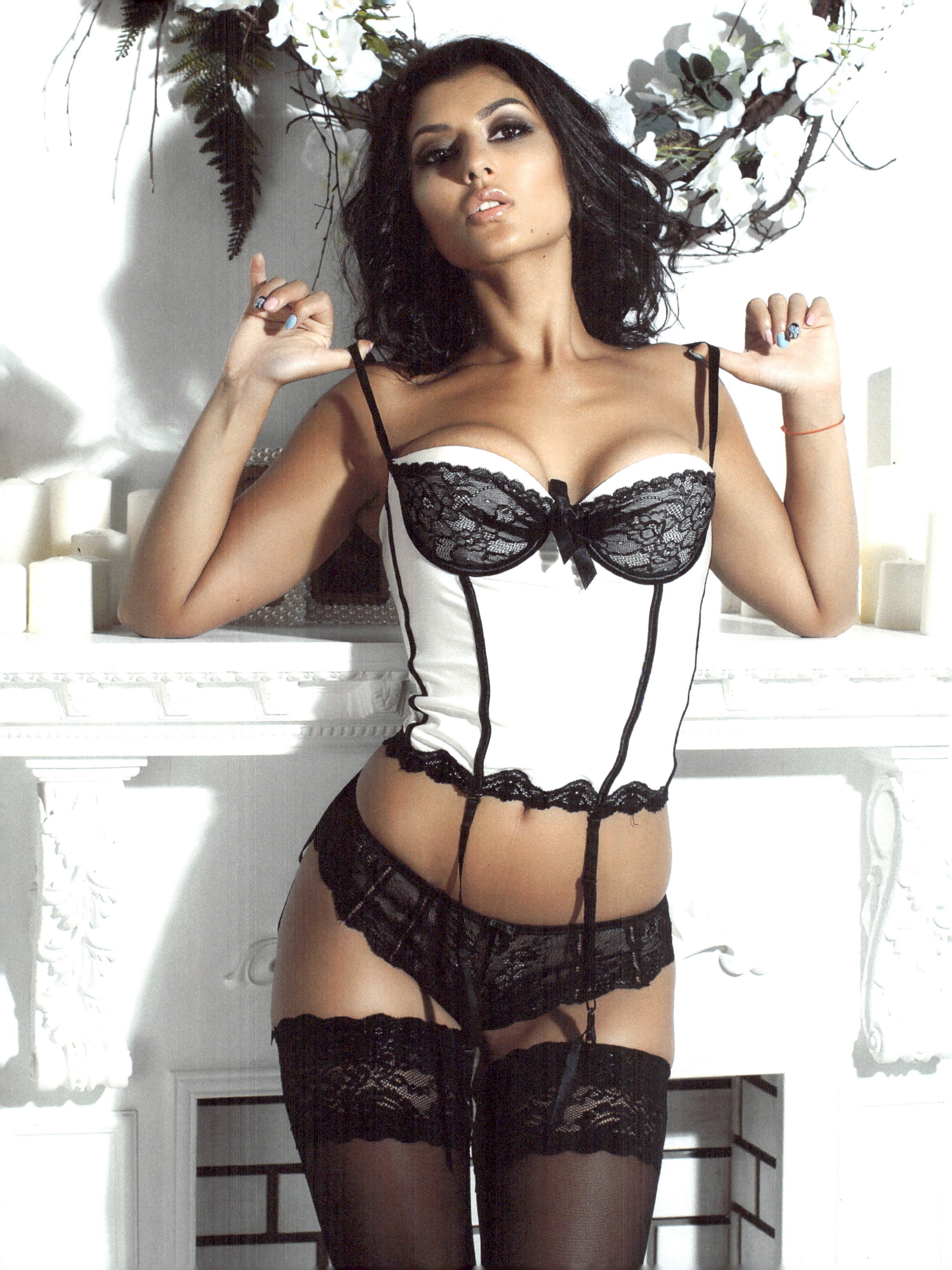

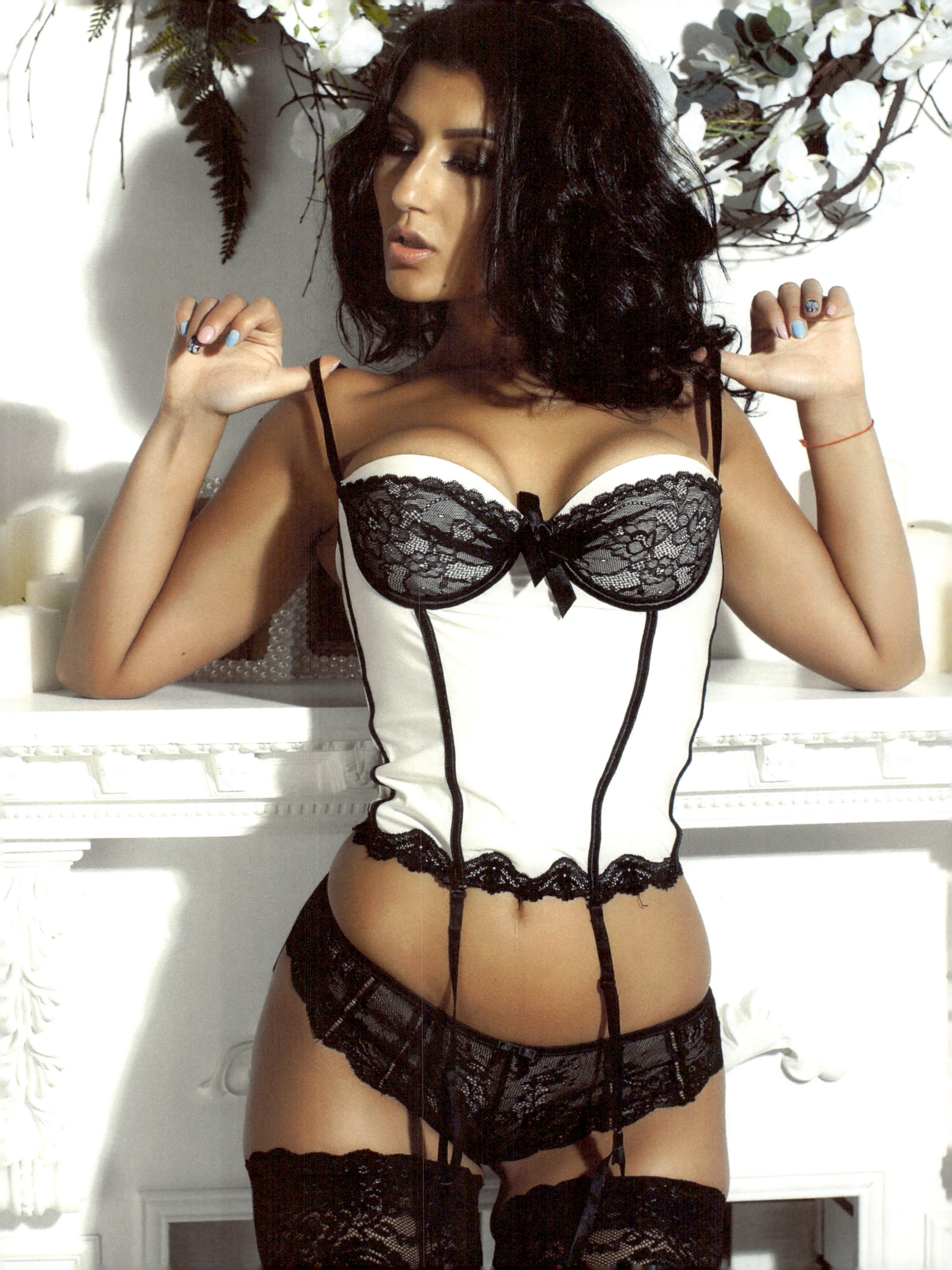

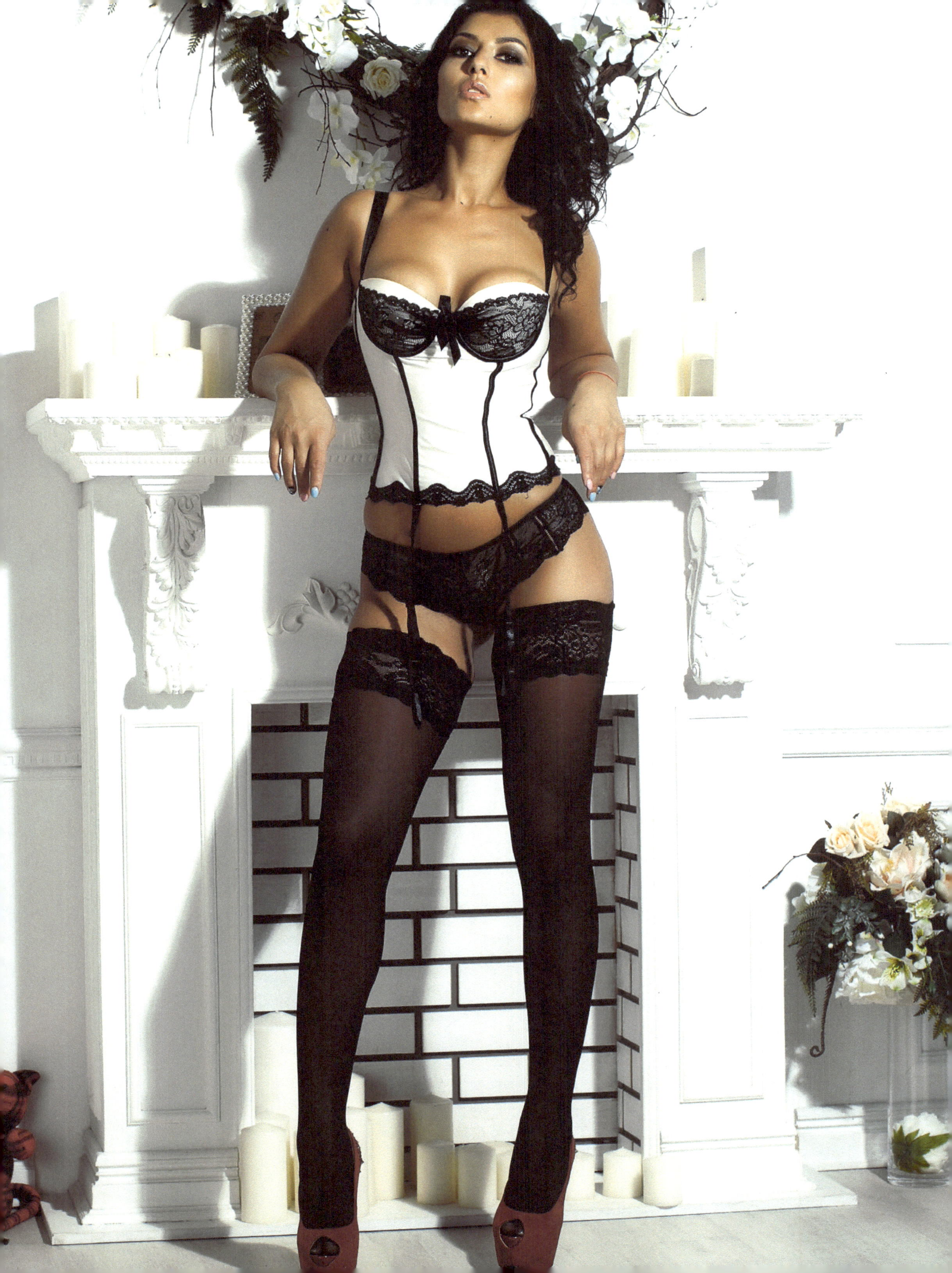

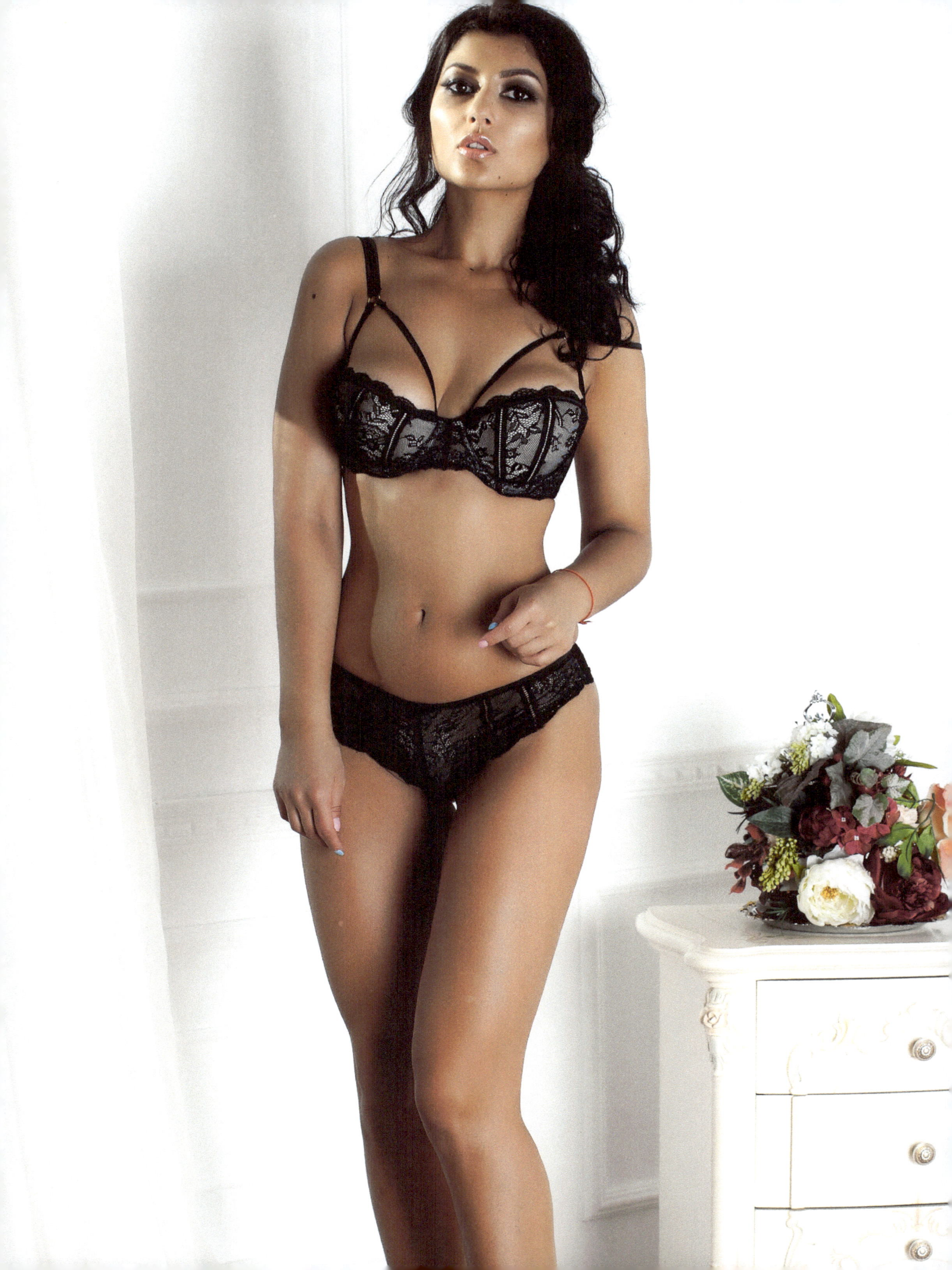

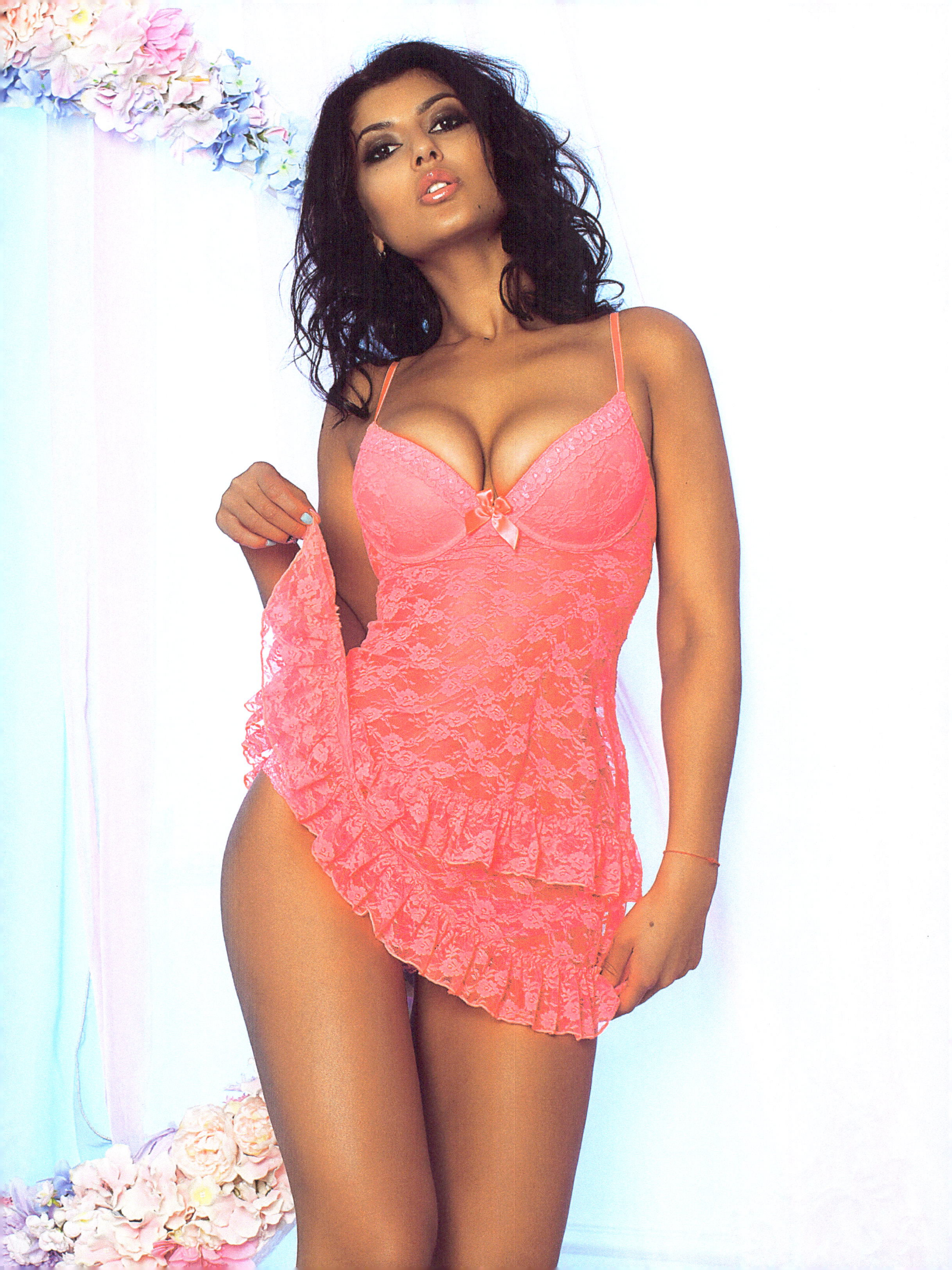

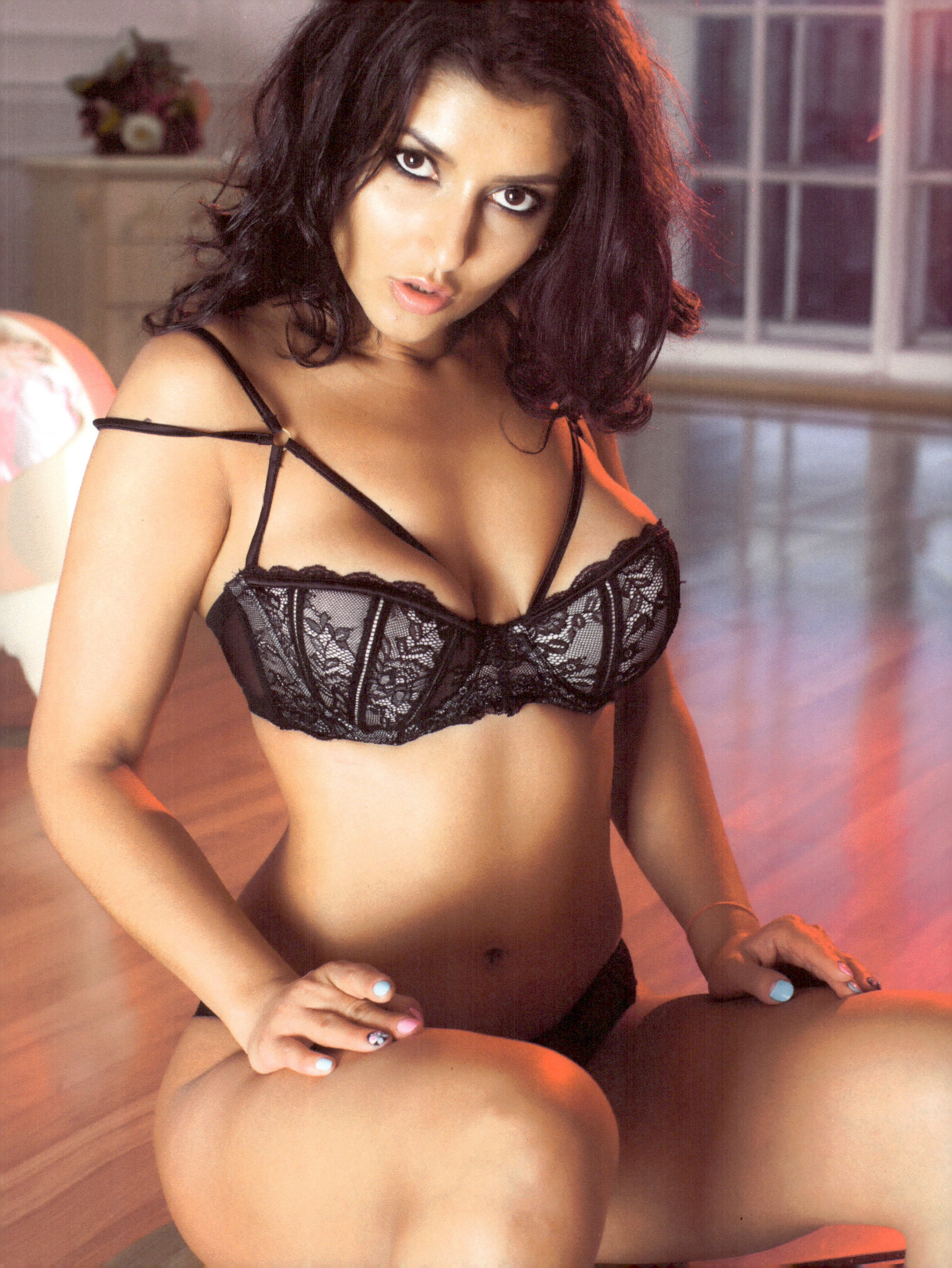

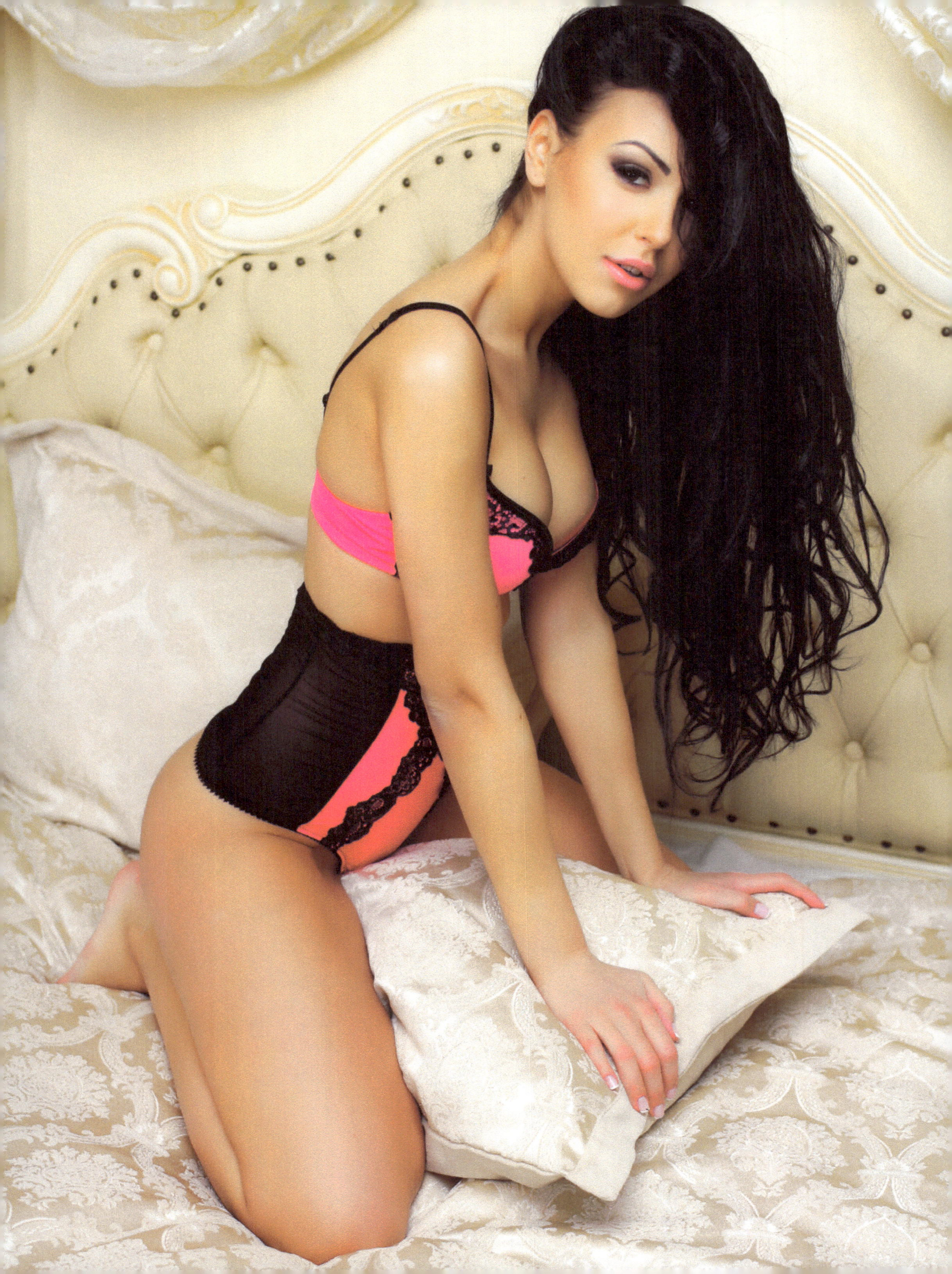

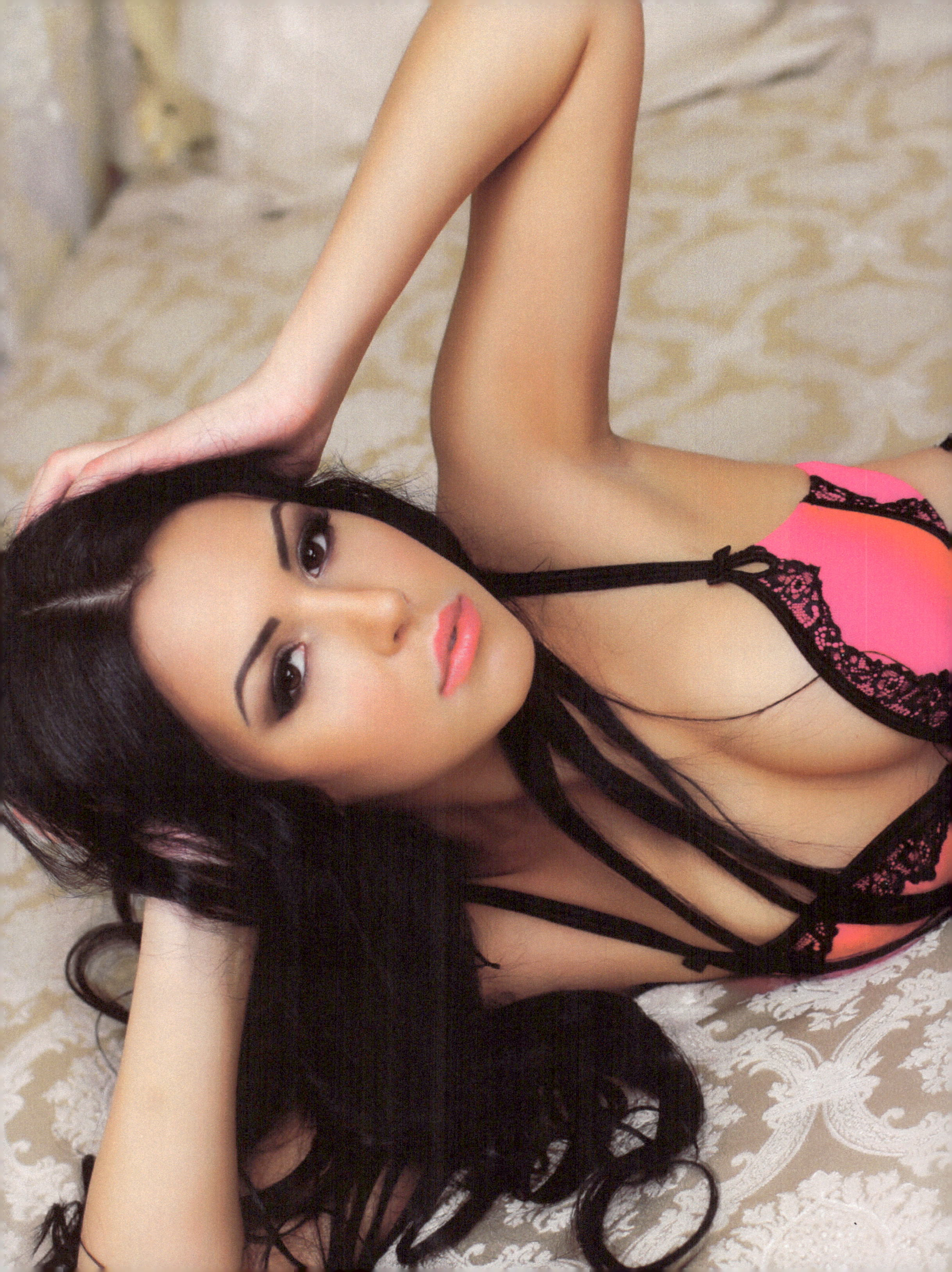

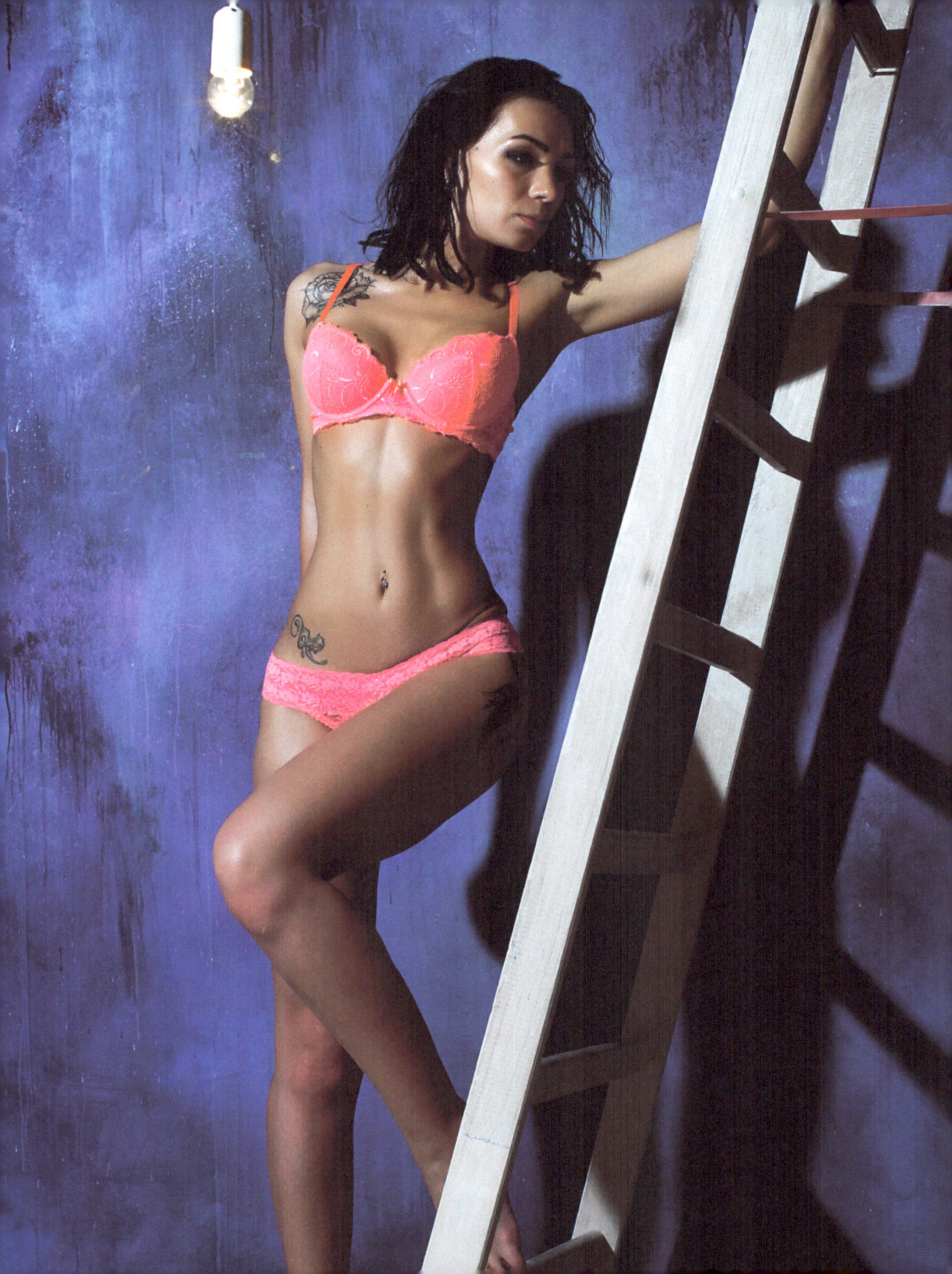

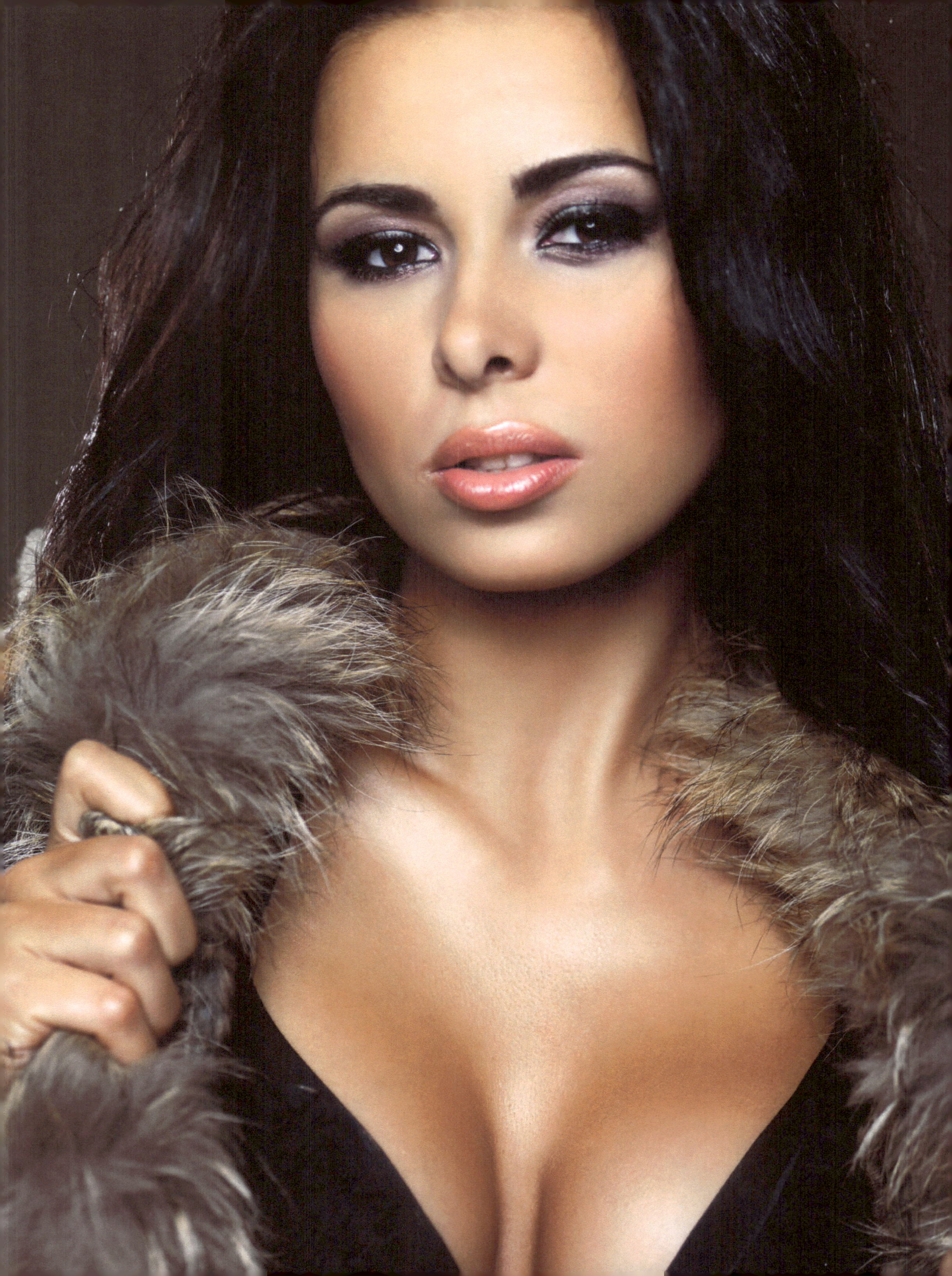

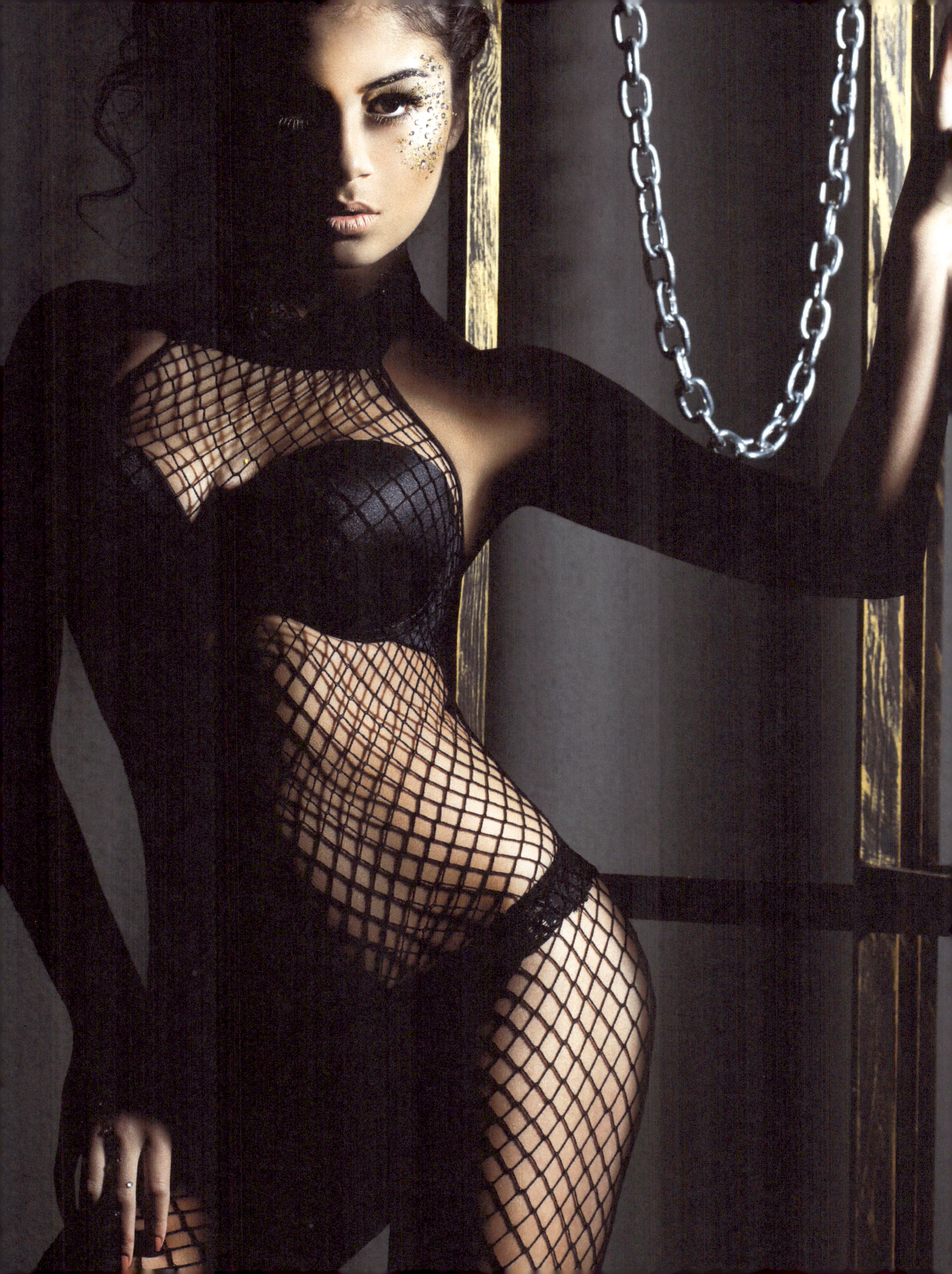

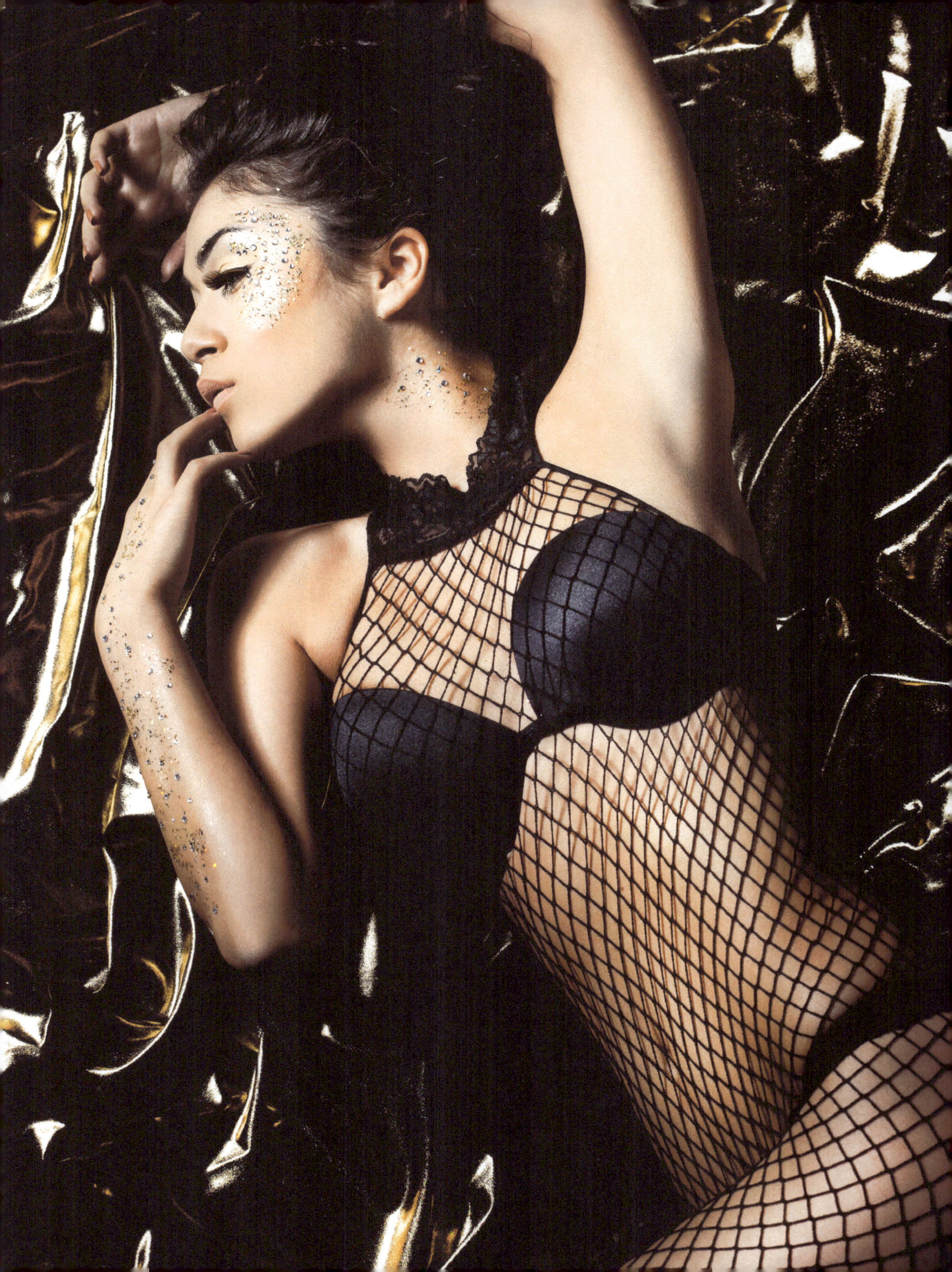

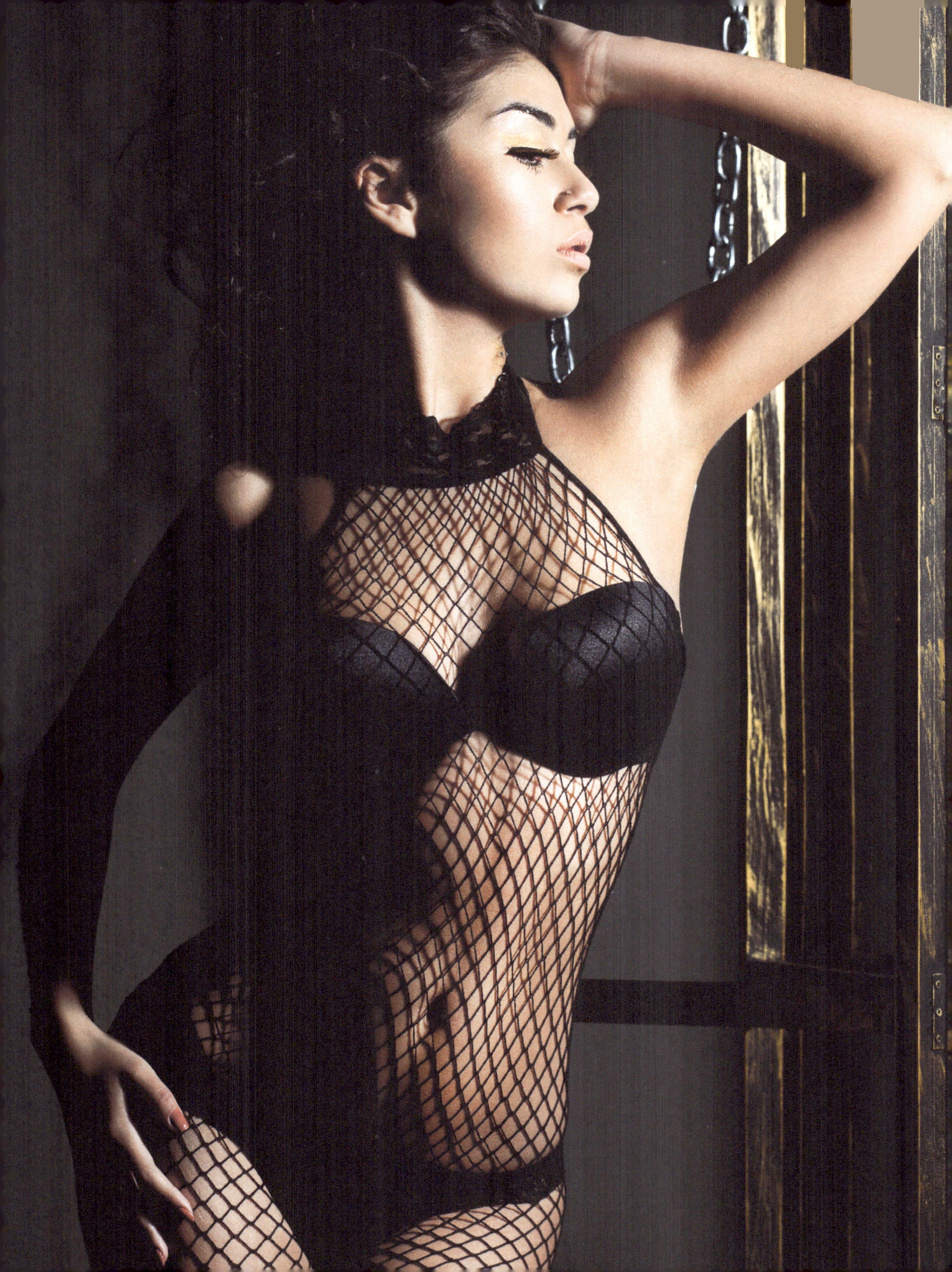

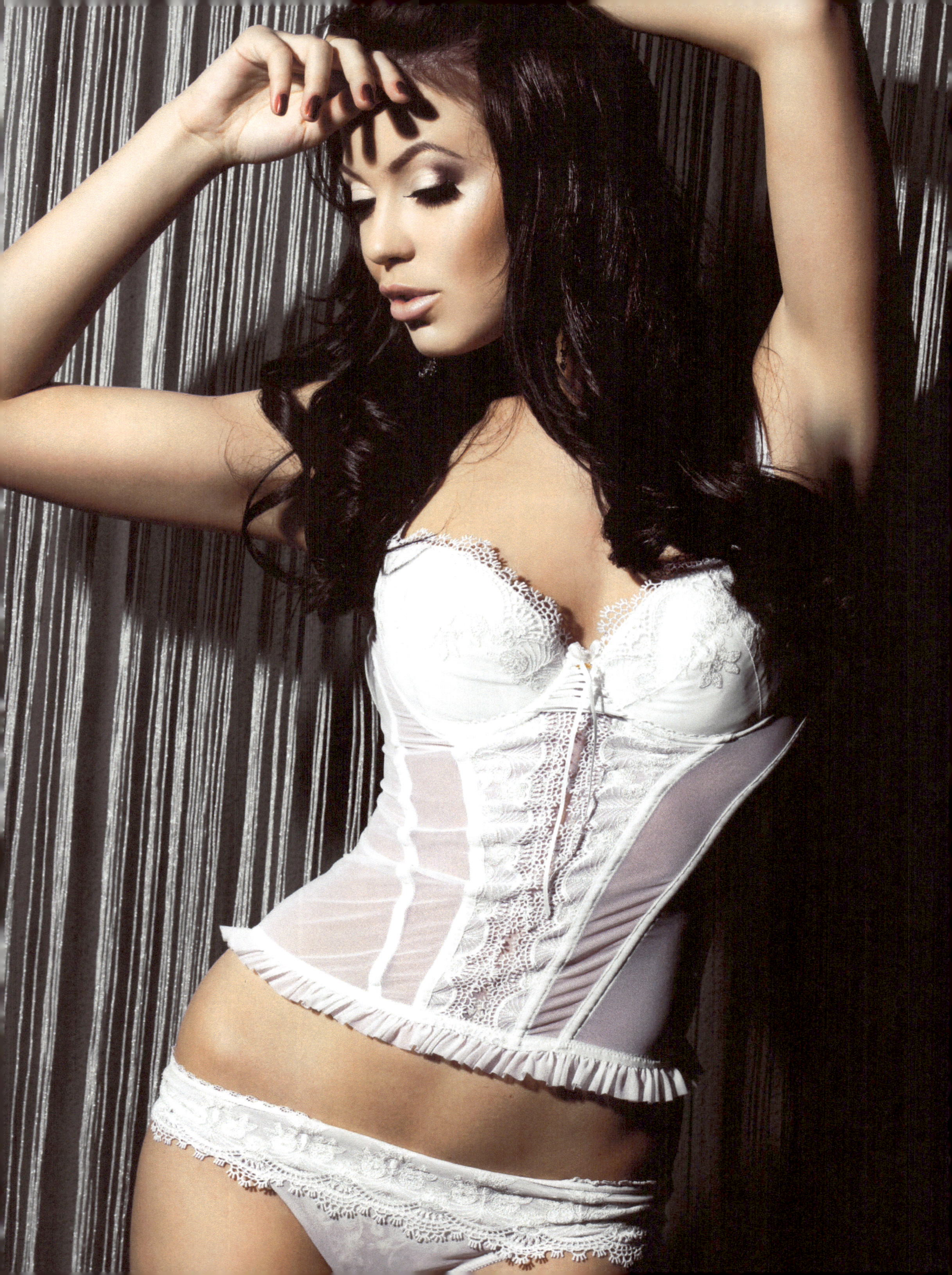

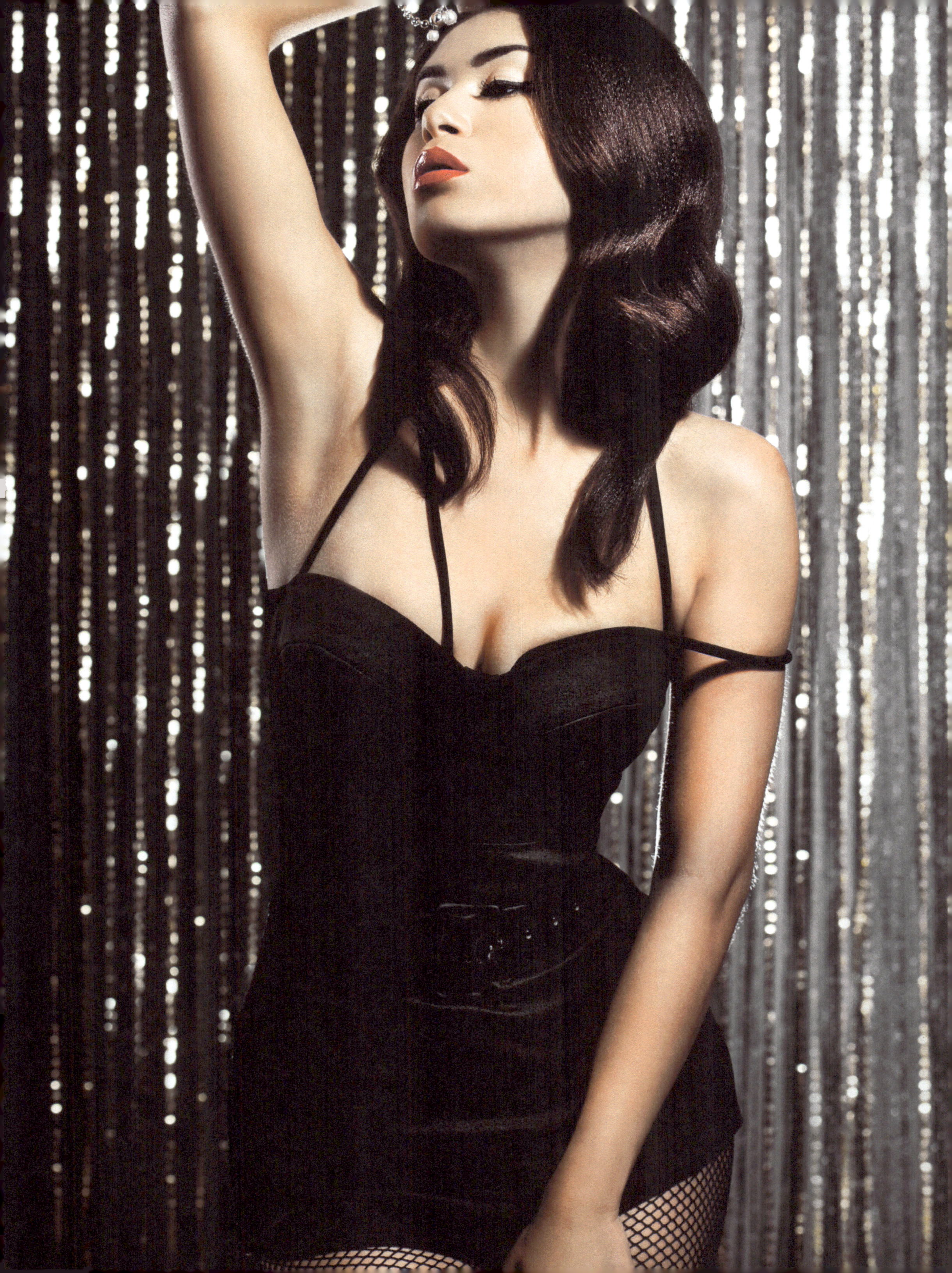

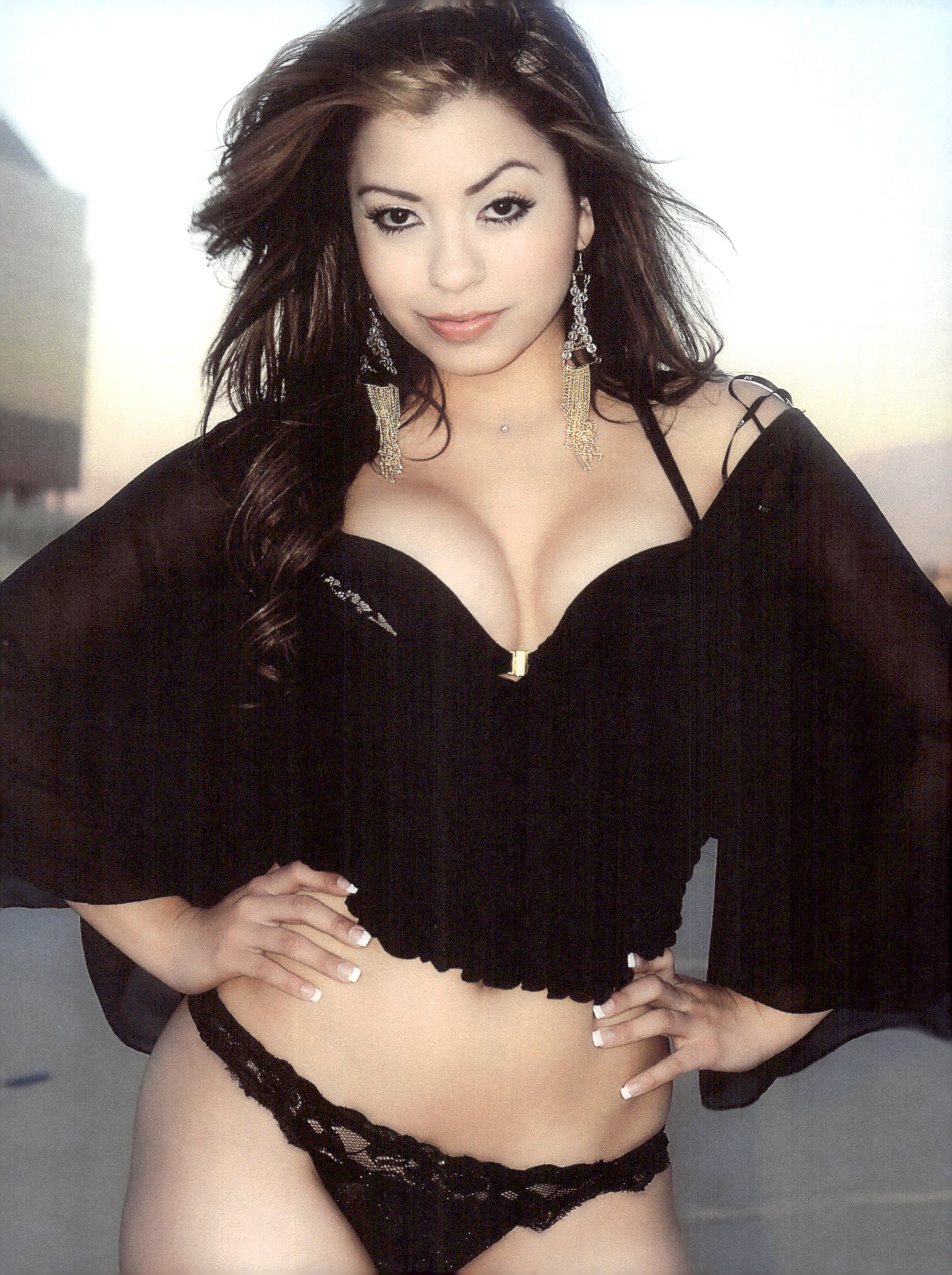

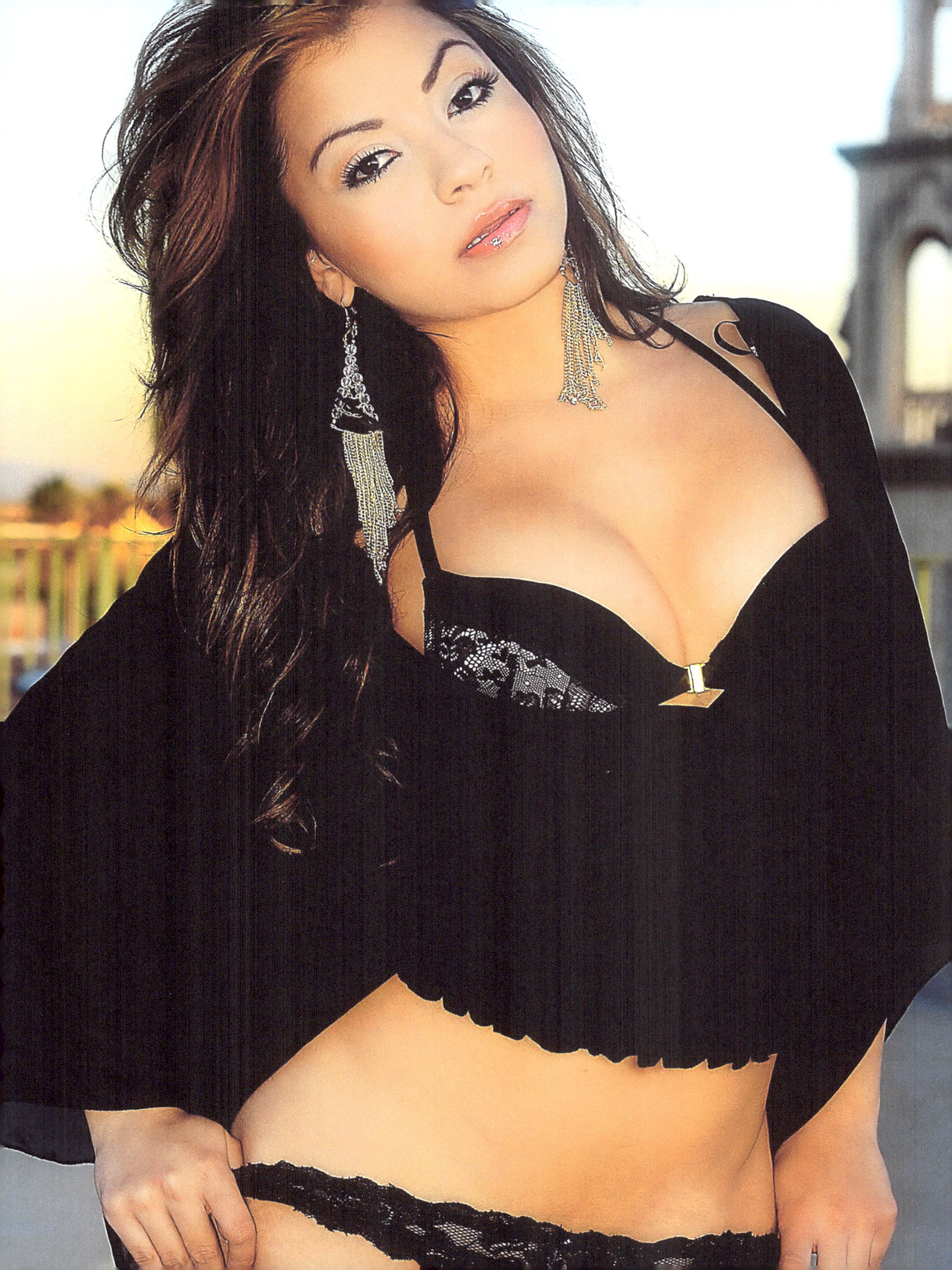

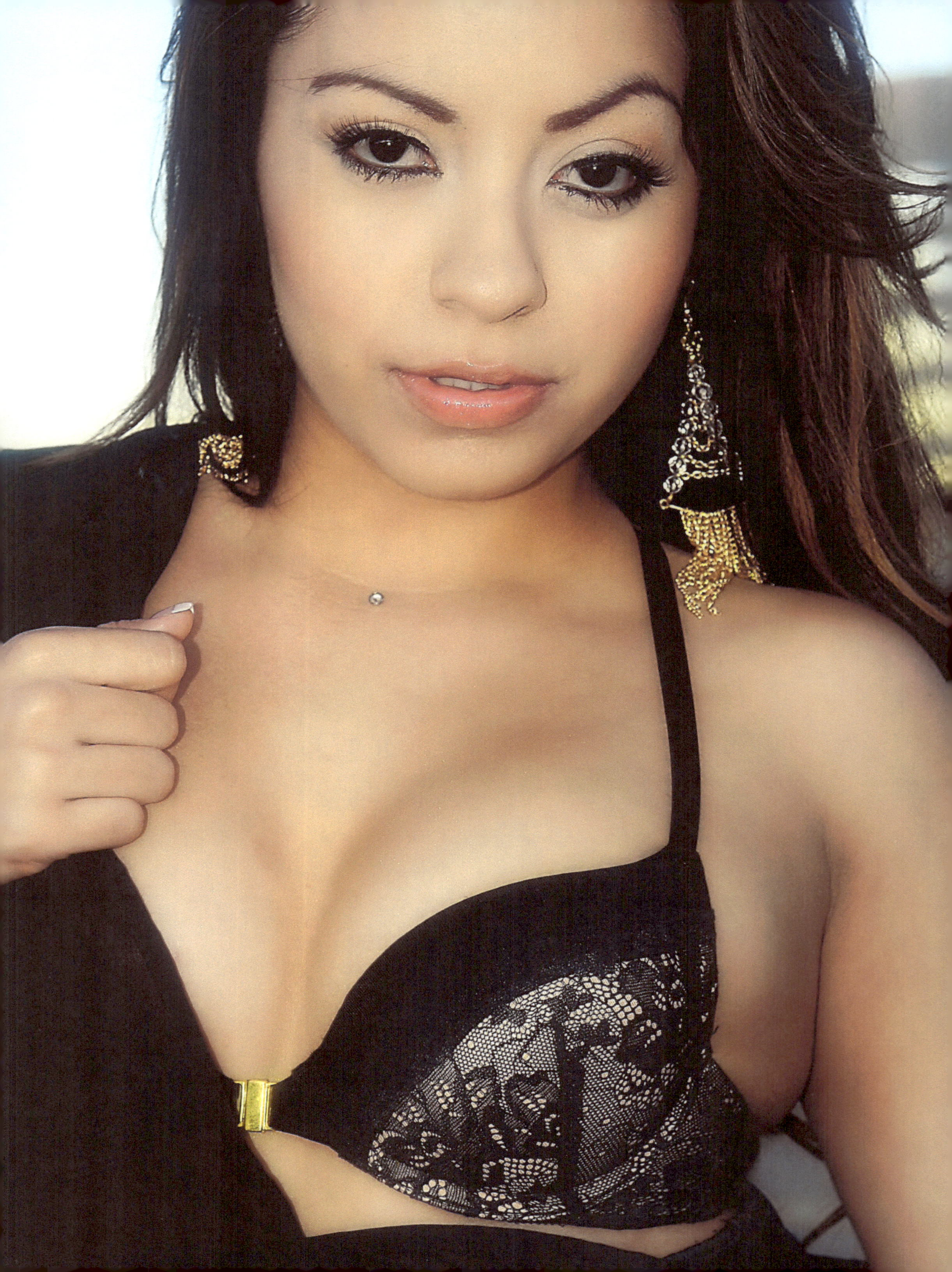

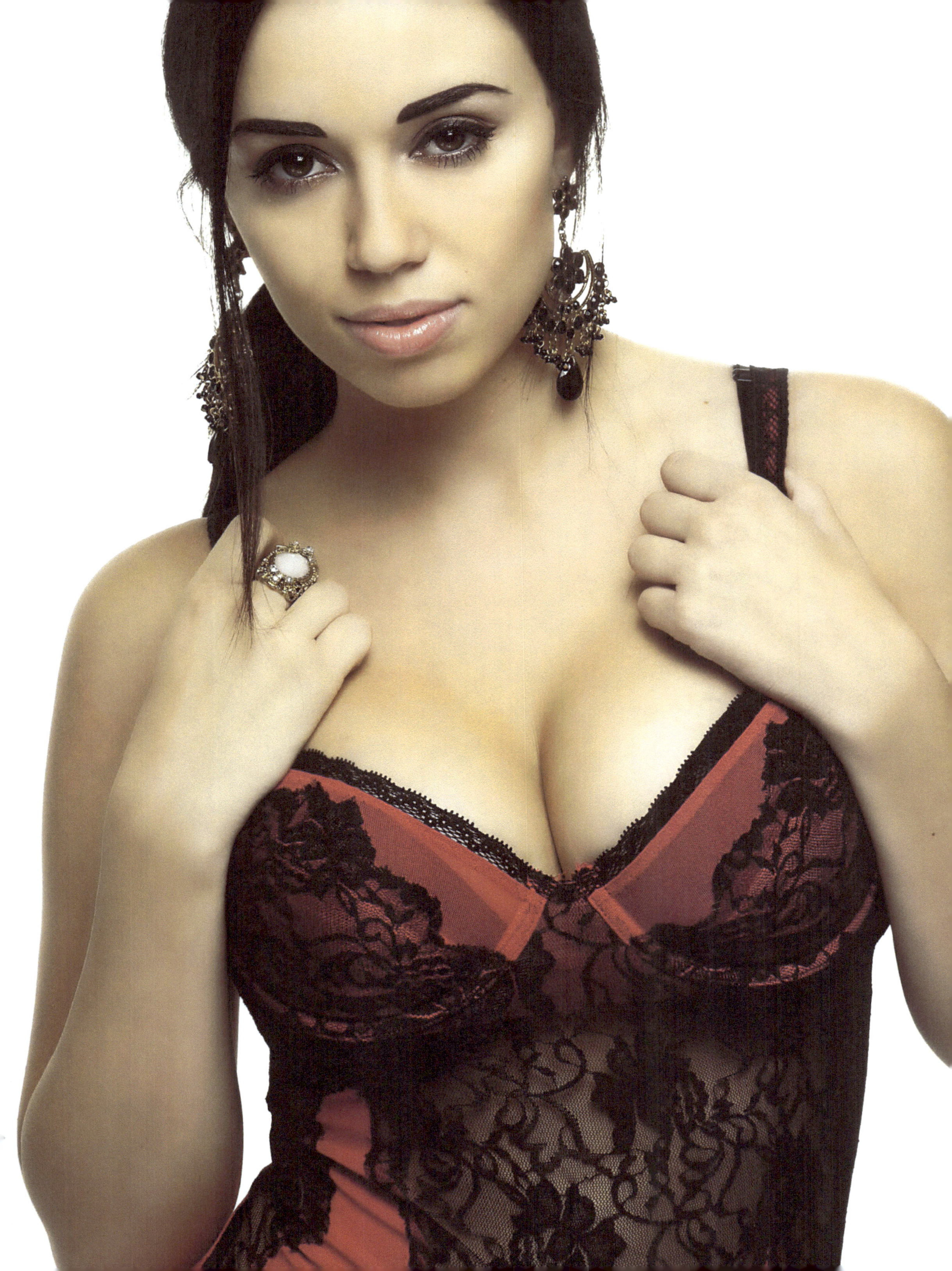

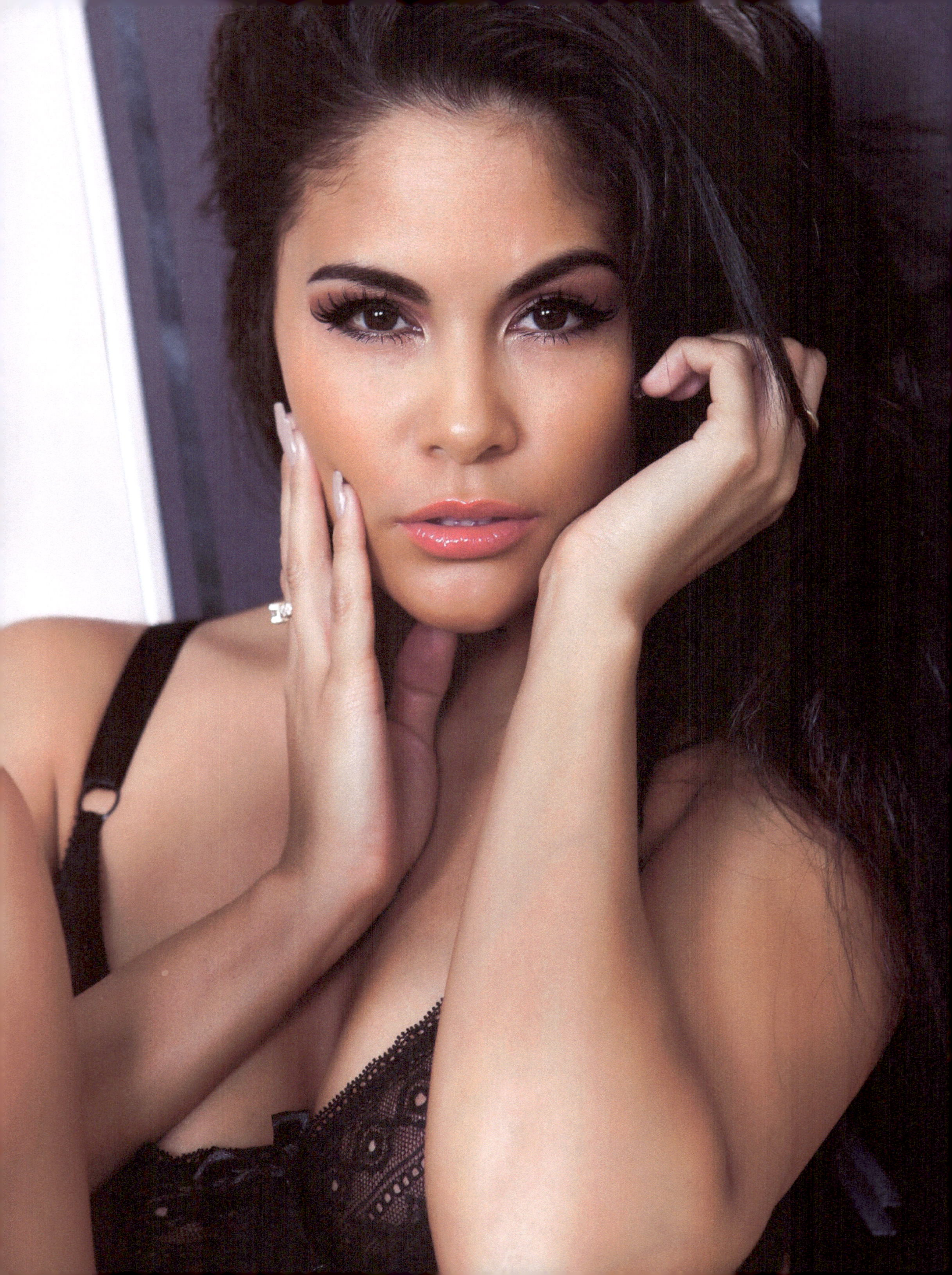

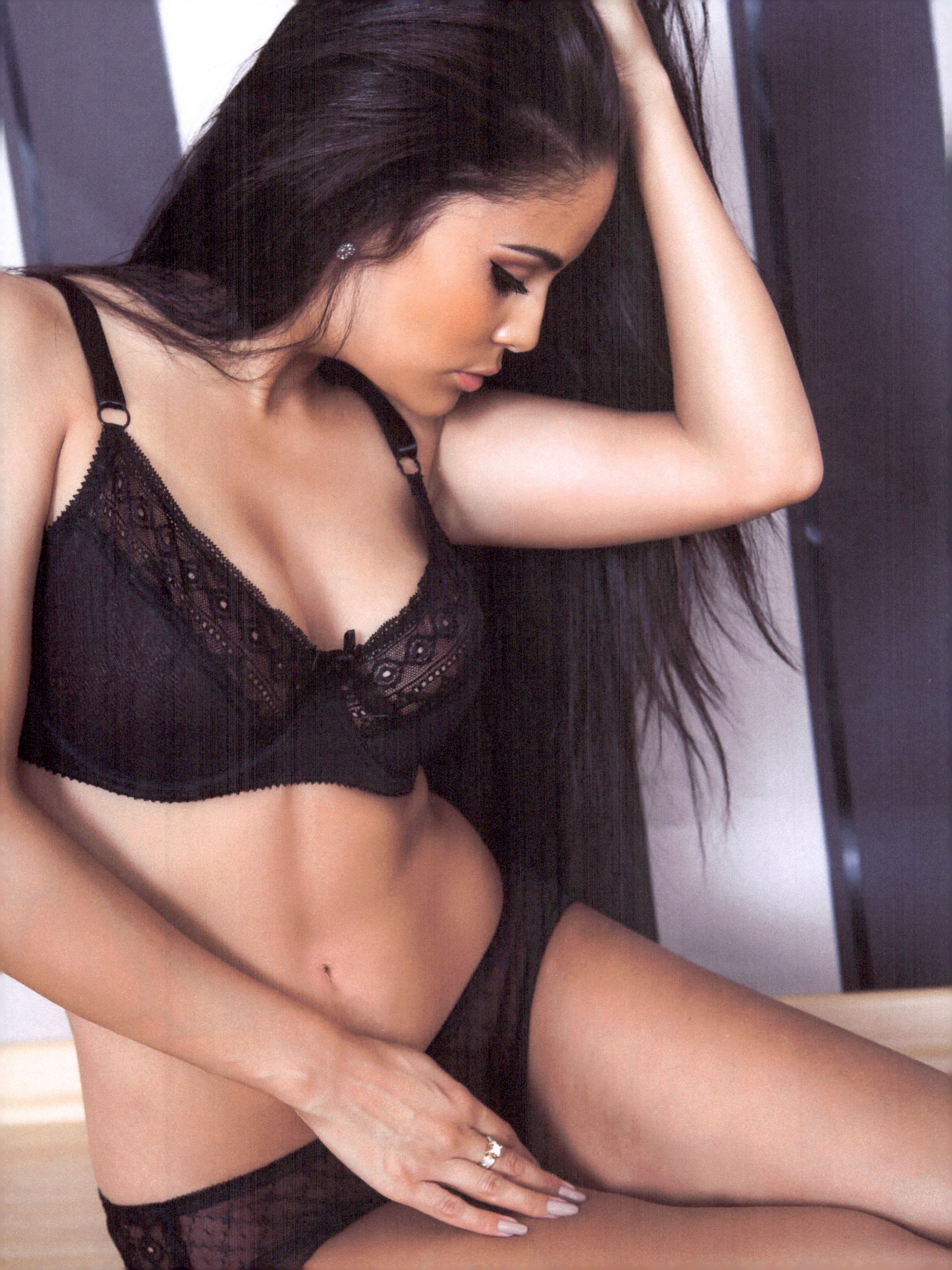

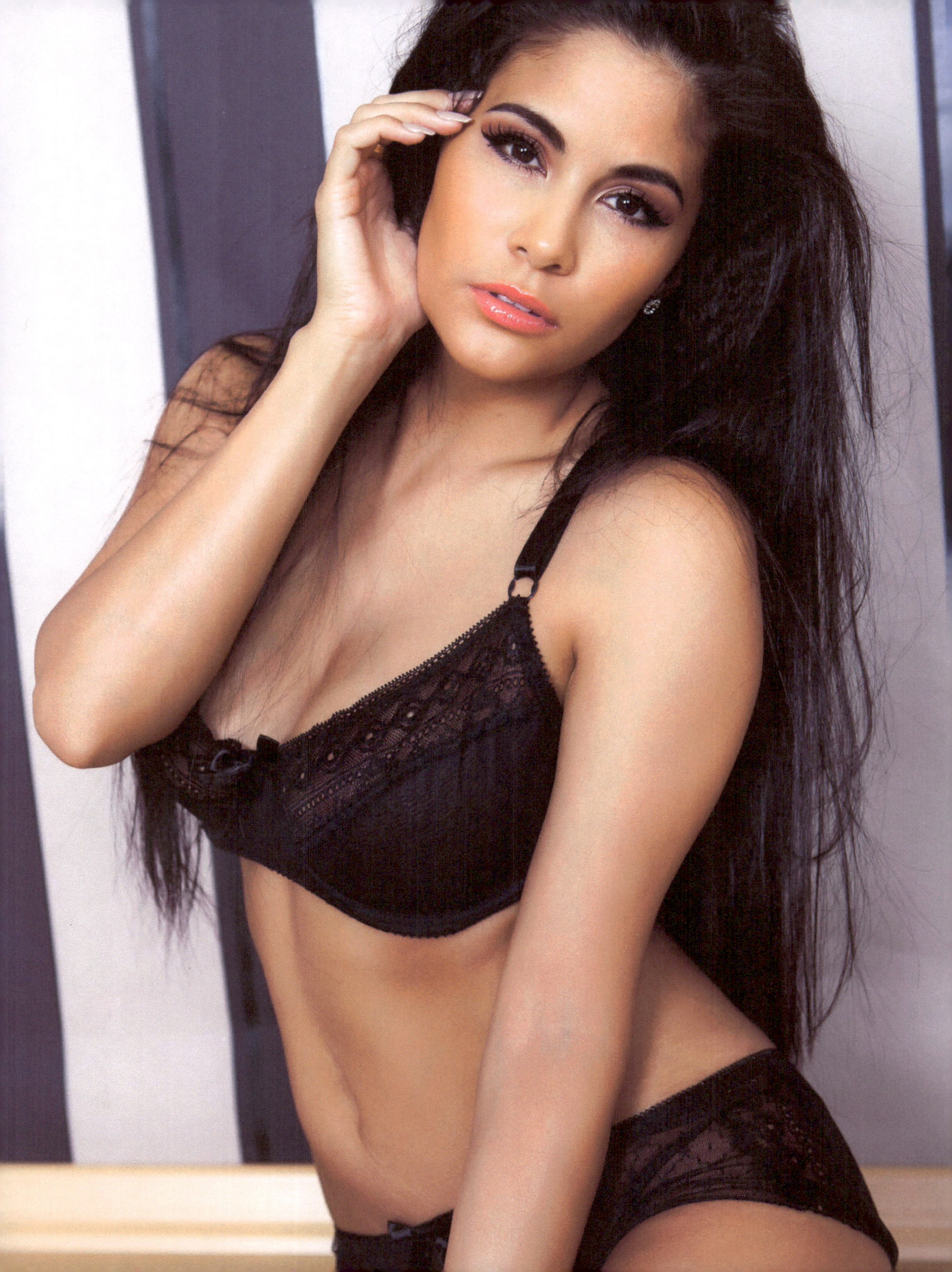

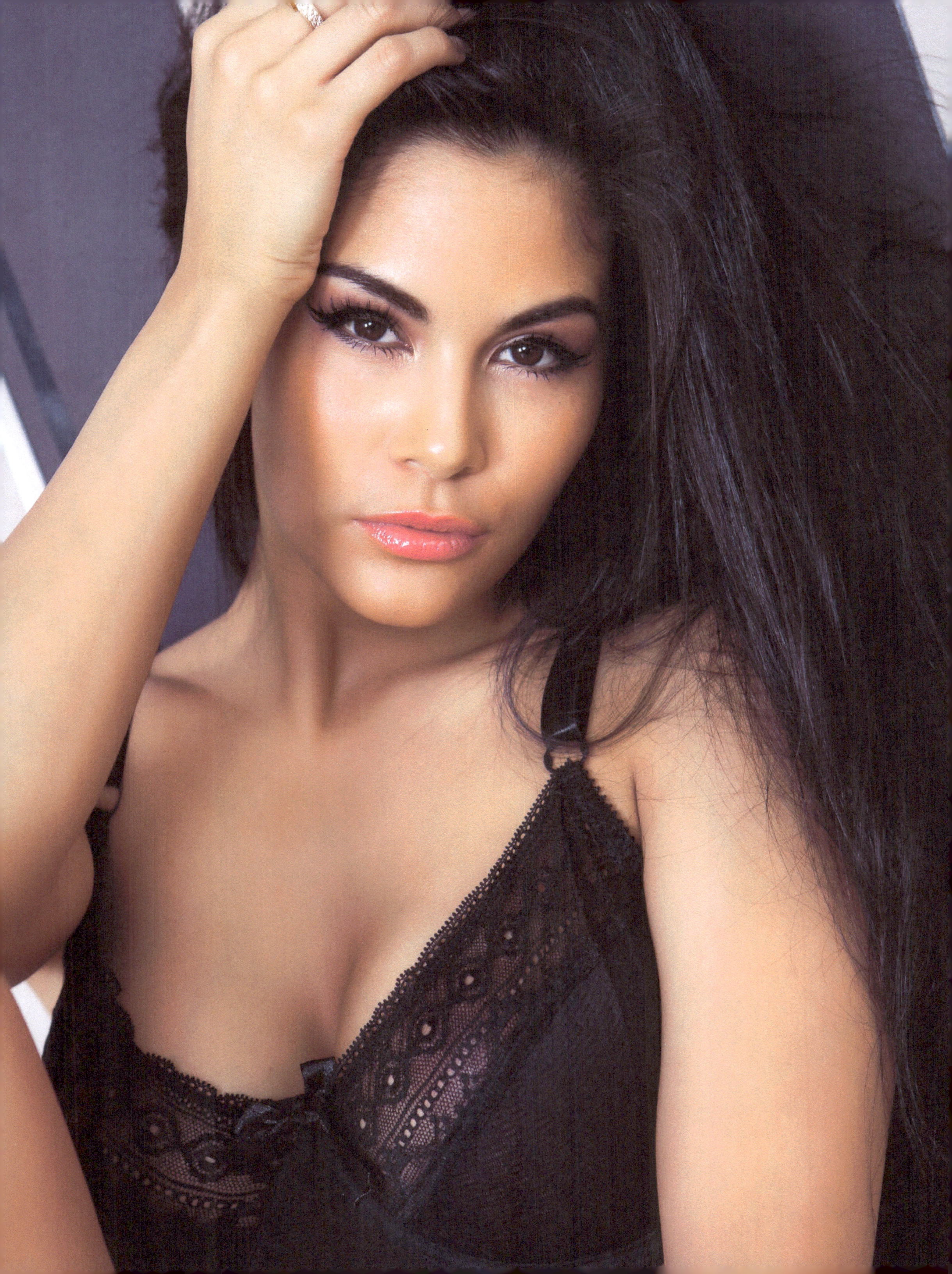

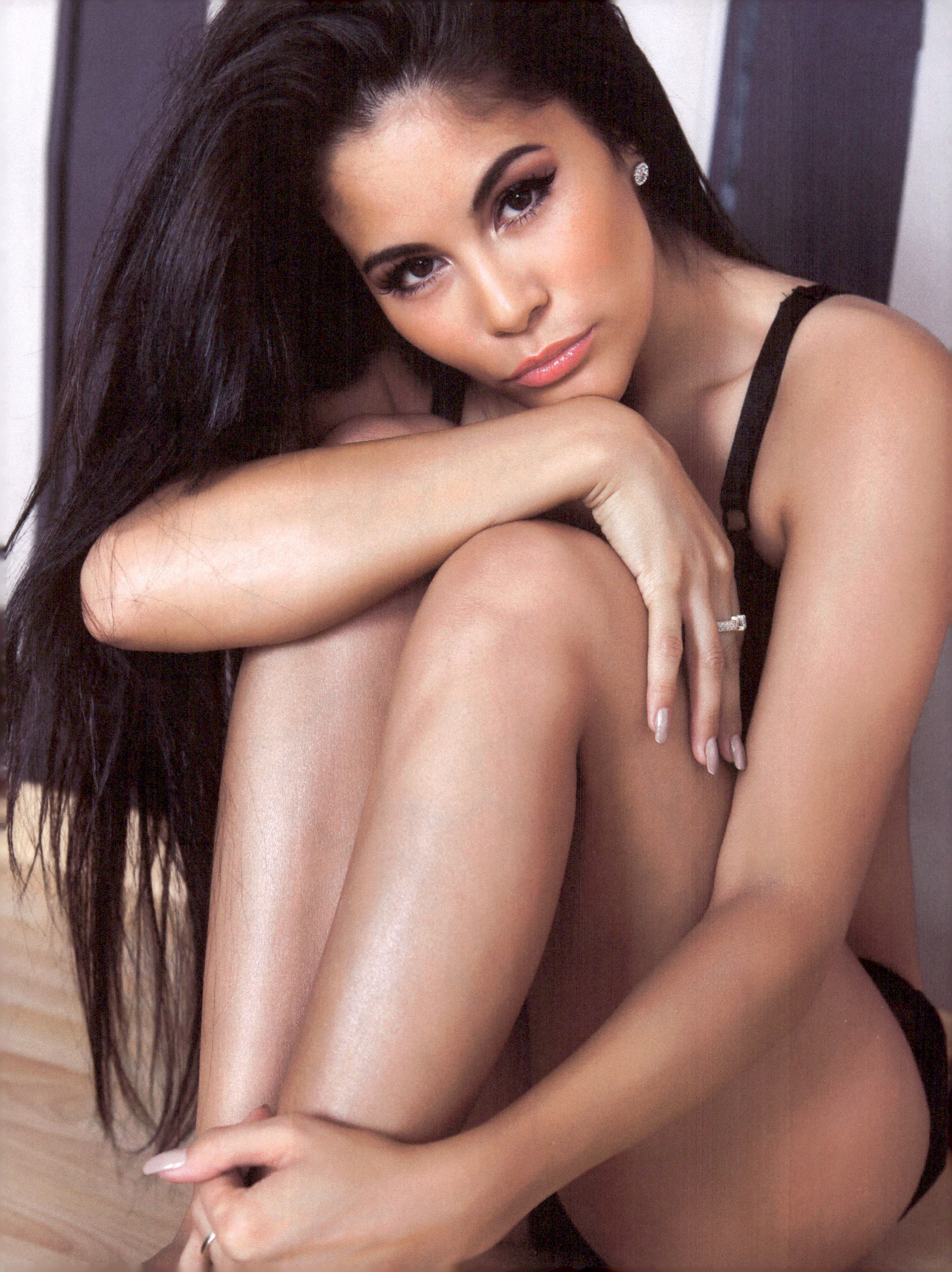

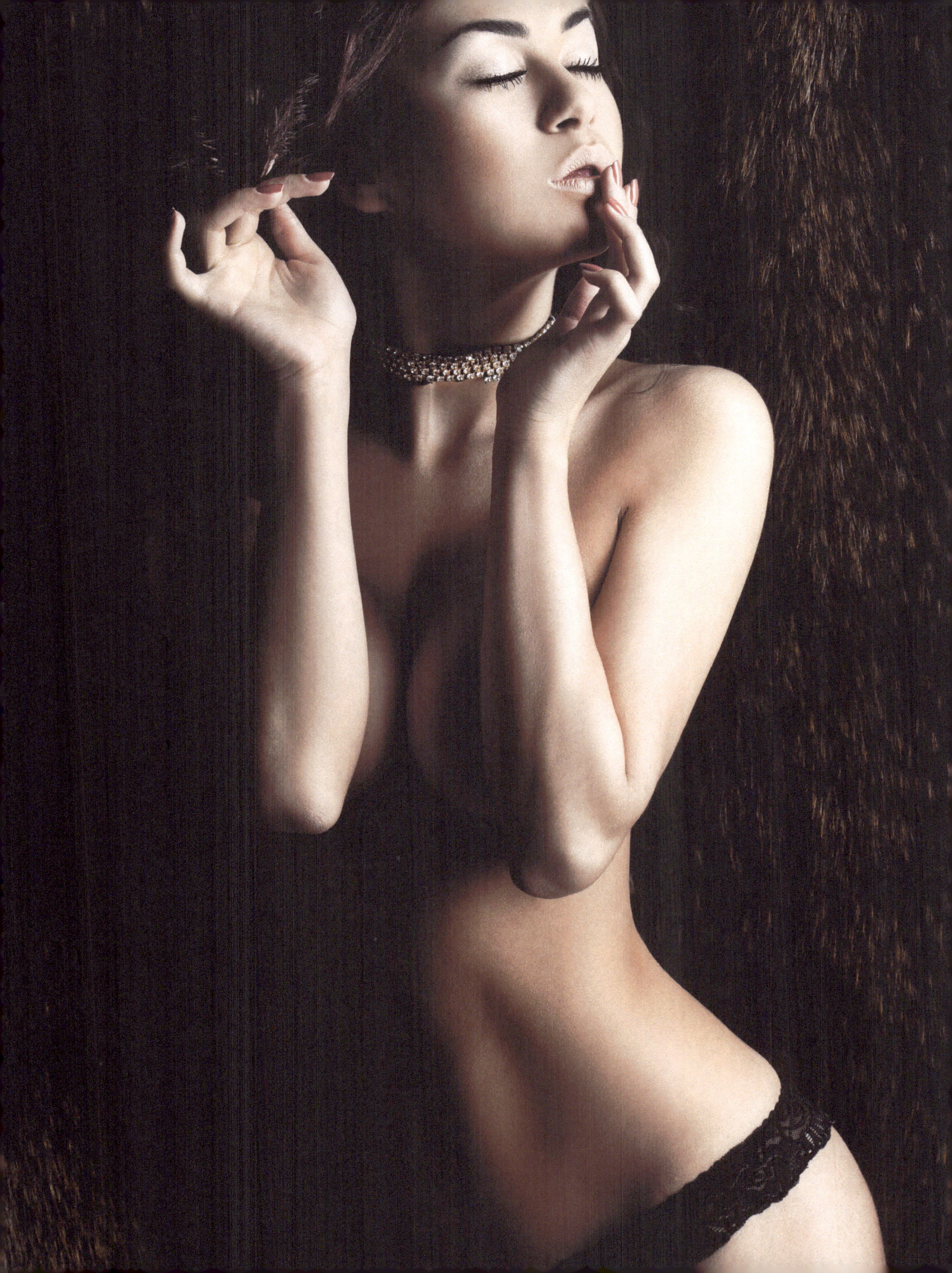

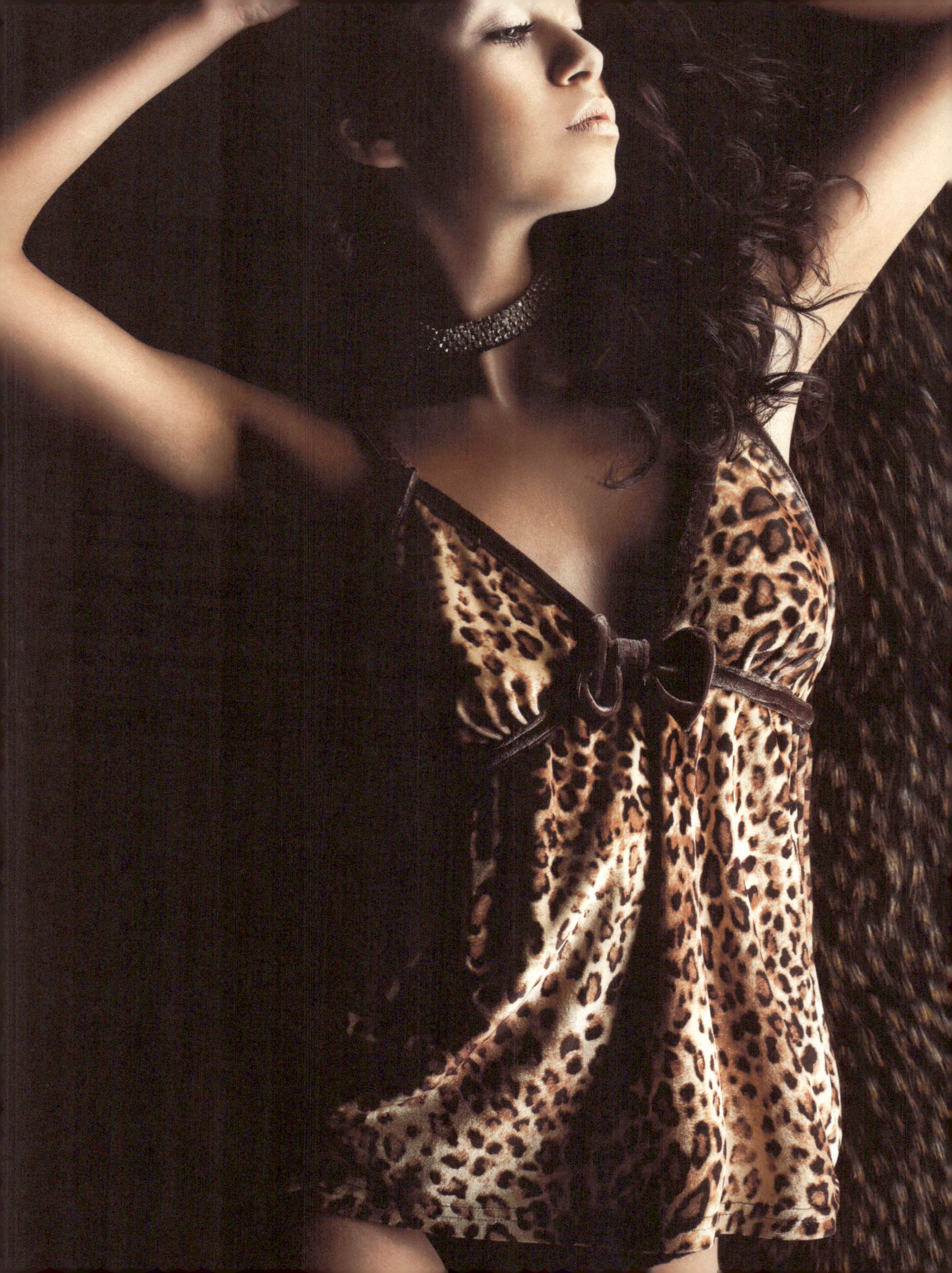

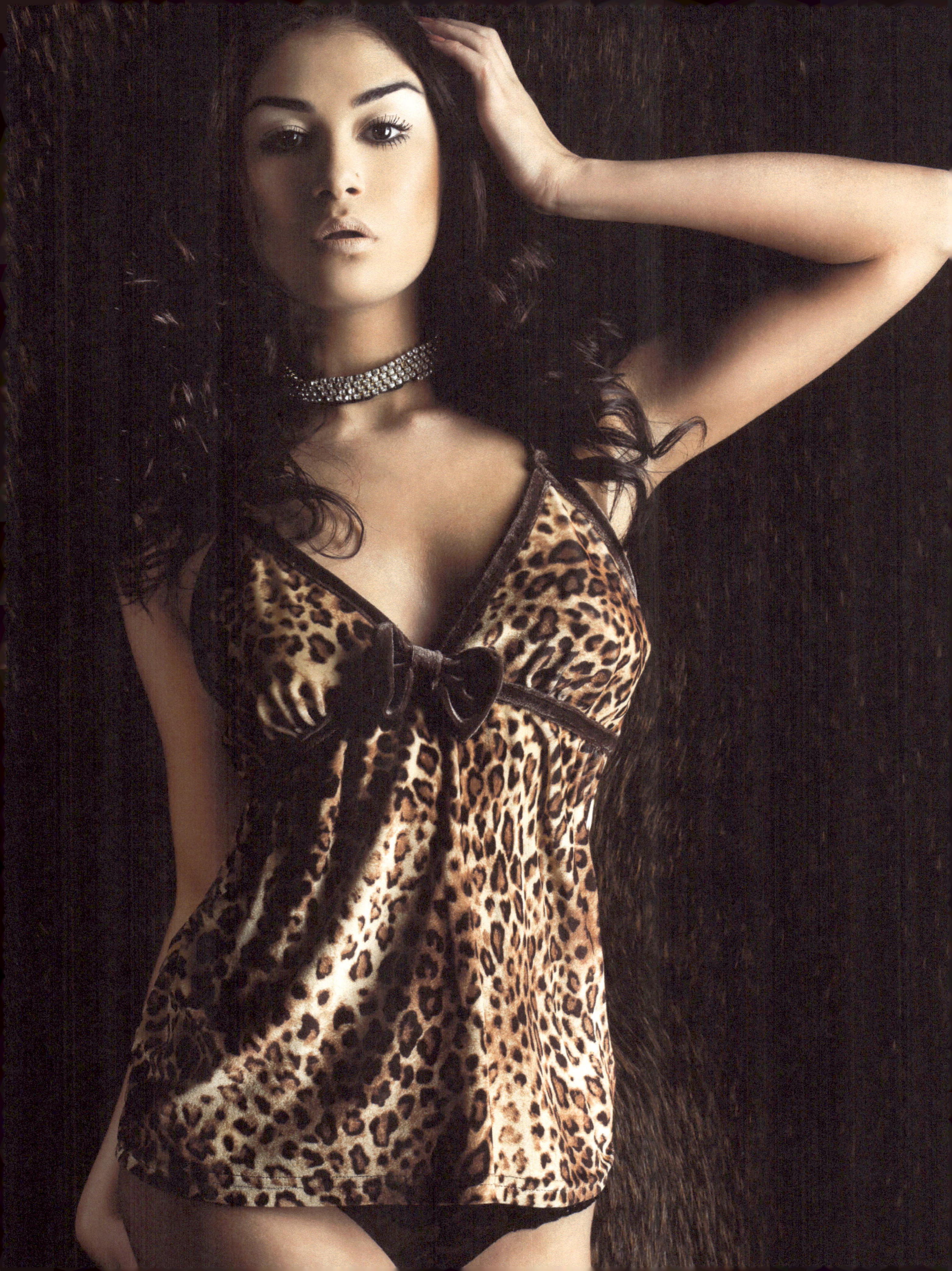

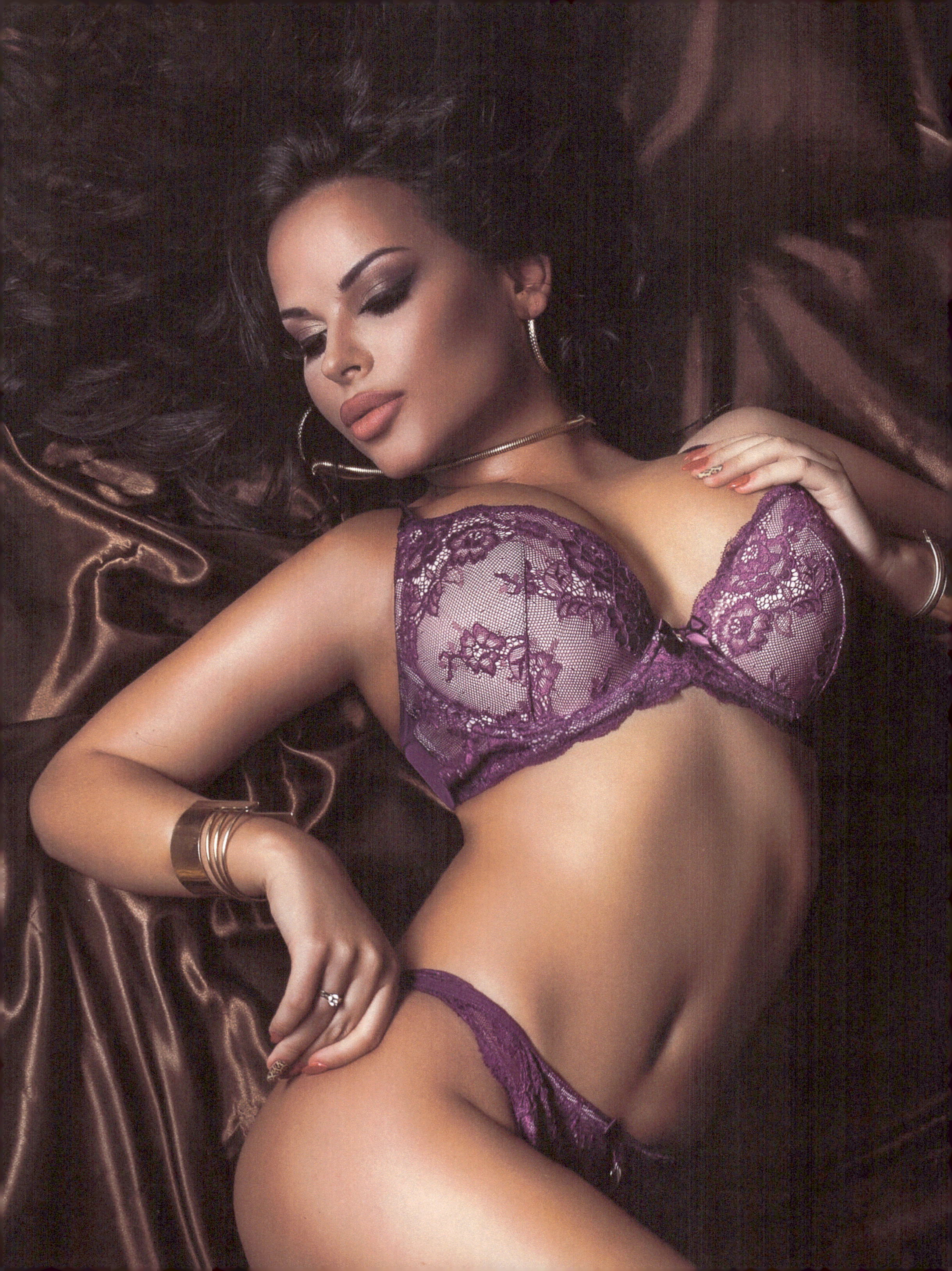

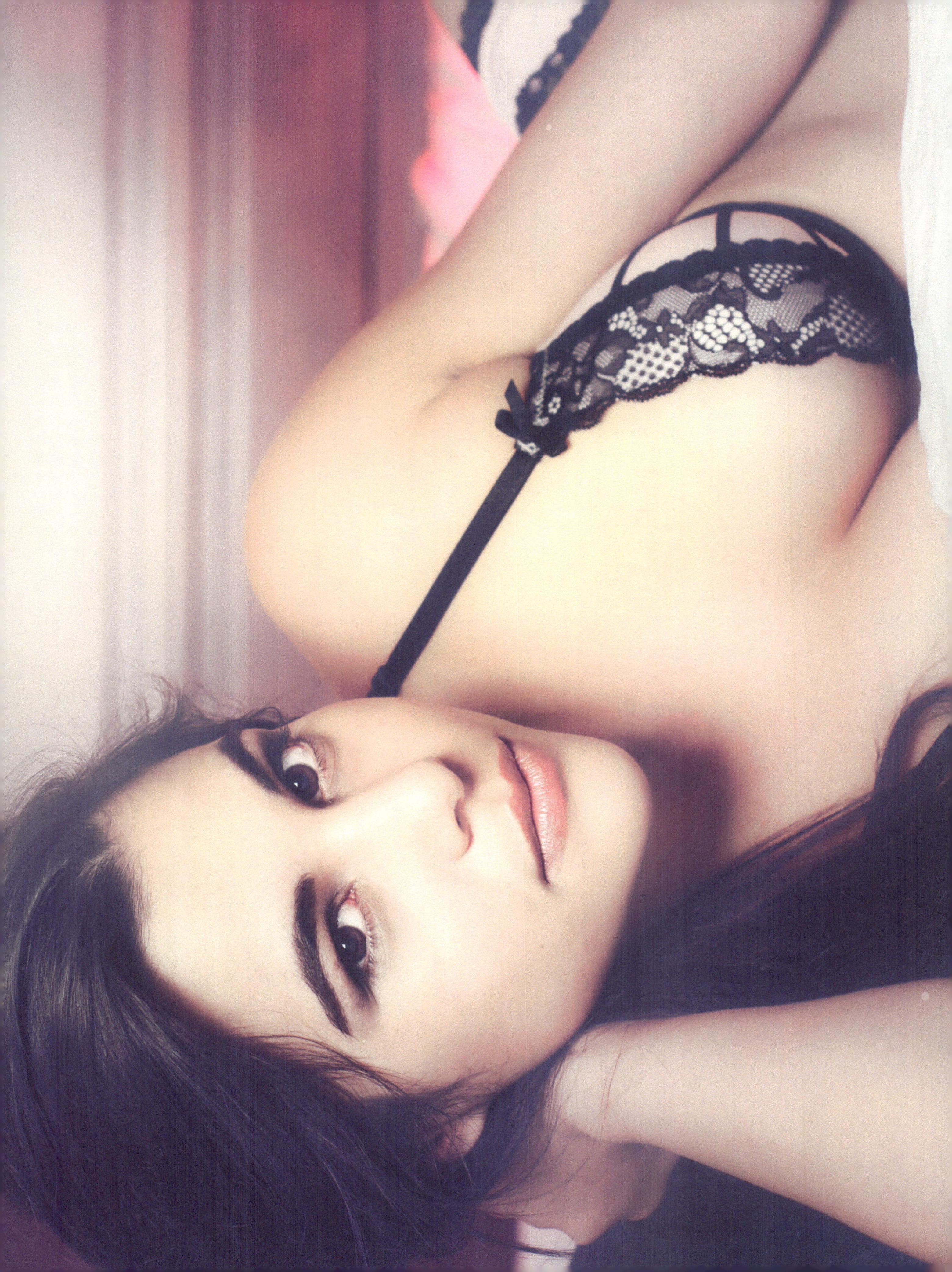

www.ingramcontent.com/pod-product-compliance
Lightning Source LLC
Chambersburg PA
CBHW050420180526
45159CB00005B/2351
9781539086444